Ha

Women of tl

Han

with contributions from Hanan Al-Shaykh,
Suhayla El-Bushra and Sara Shaarawi

Translations by Hassan Abdulrazzak

methuen | drama

LONDON · NEW YORK · OXFORD · NEW DELHI · SYDNEY

METHUEN DRAMA
Bloomsbury Publishing Plc
50 Bedford Square, London, WC1B 3DP, UK
1385 Broadway, New York, NY 10018, USA
29 Earlsfort Terrace, Dublin 2, Ireland

BLOOMSBURY, METHUEN DRAMA and the Methuen
Drama logo are trademarks of Bloomsbury Publishing Plc

First published in Great Britain 2022

Published in this edition 2022

Copyright © Hannah Khalil, 2022

Translations Copyright © Hassan Abdulrazzak, 2022

Hannah Khalil has asserted her right under the Copyright, Designs
and Patents Act, 1988, to be identified as author of this work.

Cover photograph © Johan Persson

A catalogue record for this book is available from the British Library.

A catalog record for this book is available from the Library of Congress.

ISBN: PB: 978-1-3503-8156-8
ePDF: 978-1-3503-8158-2
eBook: 978-1-3503-8157-5

Series: Modern Plays

Typeset by Mark Heslington Ltd, Scarborough, North Yorkshire

To find out more about our authors and books visit
www.bloomsbury.com and sign up for our newsletters.

Hakawatis: Women of the Arabian Nights had its world premiere at the Sam Wanamaker Playhouse, Shakespeare's Globe, on 1 December 2022 with the following cast and creative team:

Wadiha the dancer	Houda Echouafni
Fatah the young	Alaa Habib
Zuya the warrior	Laura Hanna
Akila the writer	Nadi Kemp-Sayfi
Naha the wise	Roann Hassani McCloskey

Writer   Hannah Khalil
Co-writers   Hanan Al-Shaykh, Suhayla El-Bushra and Sara Shaarawi
Director   Pooja Ghai
Assistant Designer   Maariyah Sharjil
Assistant Director   Layla Madanat
Candle Consultant   Matt Haskins
Composer   Kareem Samara
Costume Supervisor   Sabia Smith
Designer   Rosa Maggiora
Globe Associate, Movement   Glynn MacDonald
Head of Voice   Tess Dignan
Movement Director & Intimacy Director   Jess Tucker Boyd
Seasonal Voice Coach   Katherine Heath
Fight Directors   Rc-Annie Ltd

Musicians
Violin   Ayman Asfour
Oud   Kareem Samara
Percussion   Walid Zaido

Hakawatis

Women of the Arabian Nights

Characters

Fatah the young
Akila the writer
Zuya the warrior
Wadiha the dancer
Naha the wise

A note on storytelling: Stories can be told direct to the audience as monologues or in a more innovative way at the director's discretion, except for places where the form of the storytelling is specified.

* The fisherman and the jinni story should be improvised live every night by the women. They do not need to learn the story word for word as written down – rather this is an exercise in group storytelling.

** Wadiha's story could be told solely by Akila or by a mix of the women; either way it should be read from papers.

One Night

The women all hold candles to light their faces.

All   It hurts. What they do to you.

Fatah   It's planned to make you feel safe – beautiful – like everything's going to be ok. But then:

All   Rip

Cut

Pluck

Burn

Rip

Cut

Pluck

Burn /

Rip

Cut

Pluck

Burn

Rip

Cut

Pluck

Burn

Fatah   / Hands everywhere, on your body. Touching, pulling, pushing, testing, changing. Changing. Changing. Everything.

The handheld candles are blown out and a door slams – all the women suddenly turn to **Fatah** *as if she has just entered the room. She is surprised, shocked, afraid, as they inspect her.*

Wadiha   I thought we were the only ones left.

Zuya   Where did they find you, little one?

Naha   How old are you anyway?

Fatah   My name's Fatah. And I'm sixteen.

Naha   Ha! An old woman.

Wadiha   She's ready anyway.

Fatah   Ready for what?

Akila   Shaved to within an inch of her life.

Zuya (*lifting her skirt*)   Did they caramel your –

Fatah   Hey!

Wadiha   Doubt she had anything to wax yet anyway.

Akila   Where did they find her? He'll make mincemeat of her.

Naha   He'll make kibbeh of all of us.

Zuya   Not me. I'll kill him first.

Fatah   Who?

Zuya   The man who is the reason you are here. The reason we are all here.

Fatah   My fiancé?

Wadiha   Is that what they told you?

Naha   Adorable.

Akila   *Kilaab*. Sending her here without all the facts.

Fatah   What facts?

Zuya   They gave her a proper little send-off. Look at her – plucked and waxed and creamed and painted. Ready for battle. For the inevitable.

Naha   No one is ever ready for that.

Fatah Don't make fun of me. I know what to expect.

Akila How do you?

Naha Did your mother tell you?

Fatah NO! She just said to open my flower and his insect would fly in. And that it might sting.

The women laugh in derision.

Fatah But I know that's not what happens. I've talked to my friends. My cousins. I've seen pictures – in books.

Akila In books? What books?

Fatah Books from Europe.

Zuya Ha! They don't know about such things there.

Fatah Babies are born in Europe too.

Naha Teach us, little one. What are we to expect?

Wadiha As if *you* don't know. You can't have got to your age without experiencing –

Naha Let her speak.

They all listen with interest.

Fatah Well . . .

Zuya She knows nothing – she is a child!

Fatah I DO!

Wadiha Then tell us. We won't laugh.

Fatah Well . . . First come lips. pressing lips.

Akila Pilgrims.

Fatah Kisses. Tongues. Wet. Then hands.

Akila Profane.

Fatah Caresses. Moving down.

Akila   Unworthy.

Fatah   Down. Under. In. Between.

Zuya   And are you vertical or horizontal at this point?

Wadiha   Shush, Zuya, I'm enjoying this.

Fatah   On the bed. pressed together. Into each other. Then he takes it out.

Naha   His manhood.

Wadiya   His snake.

Akila   His column.

Naha   His weapon.

Zuya   His cock. His penis.

Fatah   And gently pushes it /

Zuya   / gently?!

Fatah   In between your legs.

A beat.

Zuya   And

Akila   then

Wadiya   what?

Fatah   He lets it all out.

Naha   Just like that.

Fatah   See – I do know.

Naha   Just like that?

Fatah   No not just like that – he moves in and out. Gently.

Zuya   He's very gentle this one.

Fatah   And the movement makes a tide, a –

Zuya   Yes

Fatah   swelling tide

Wadiya   Yes

Fatah   that rises

Naha   Yes

Fatah   and rises

Akila   Yes

Fatah   and grows

Zuya   Yes

Fatah   from my core

Wadiya   Yes

Fatah   to my toes

Naha   Yes

Fatah   through my body.

Akila   Yes

Fatah   Electric.

All   YES!

Fatah   And then

Zuya   then

Wadiya   then

Naha   then

Fatah   It's over.

Naha   Not quite . . .

All eyes are on **Naha**.

Naha   Then he gets off. Rolls off. Breath heavy. Somewhere else. Other. Not here. Not with you. He gets up slowly – like a man drunk. Unsteady. And he straightens. Perhaps he wipes himself. Pulls on something to cover him. Perhaps he doesn't bother. But he definitely goes to the table – goes and picks up a blade. It shines. Like the moon. Like a diamond in the night. Sparkles. Reflects your eyes. And he raises it over you. Like the crescent over the minaret. And holds for a moment. Before it all comes crashing down . . . everything ends. And you spill – everywhere. (*A beat.*) Another set of silk sheets are ruined.

A beat.

Fatah   Are you saying he's going to kill me?

Wadiya   All of us.

Zuya   Not me.

Akila   He won't stop until he's killed

Naha   all of us.

Fatah   NOBODY TOLD ME IT WOULD BE LIKE THIS. I WASN'T WARNED. IT'S NOT FAIR.

Naha   Don't be scared – death comes to all of us.

Wadiya   That just depends what order we go in.

Fatah   BUT – Are you all to marry him? The King? Not just me?

Zuya   Think you were special did you?

Wadiya   We're all that's left. He's been marrying women, girls – whatever – taking them to bed – and then killing them . . . for weeks.

Akila   Months.

Zuya   Years. So many dead – gone before us . . .

All the women look to the audience with sadness and remembrance – they see them as the souls of the women who have gone before.

Pause.

Fatah   And we're the only women left?

Naha   Exactly.

Fatah   What about my *teta* – and my aunties?

Naha   Too old – for this task. It's just the young healthy ones.

Zuya   Healthy-ish.

Naha *shoots her a look.*

Akila   How have you not heard?

Fatah (*fearful*)   Who will be next?

Wadiya   I don't know.

Akila   Maybe we should draw straws.

Zuya   I'll go first. And before he can touch me I'll pick up his sword and slice him into pieces – feed him to the dogs.

Wadiya   And then his guards will come in and arrest you and you'll be executed. Great plan.

Zuya   You have a better idea?

Wadiya   I do as a matter of fact. I will hypnotise him.

Naha   With what?

Wadiya   My hips.

Akila   Haven't you heard of her – she's a famous dancer.

Fatah   Really?

Akila   That's her story anyway. But she refuses to show us.

Wadiya   There are always men watching. Peeking. And this dance is not for them. It's meant to lubricate the joints for childbirth. Not fulfil some Orientalist's fantasy.

Zuya   The King's a man.

Wadiya   Yes and when I dance for him he will be my husband – so it will be ok.

Naha   Without us seeing it we can't be sure if this dance is up to the task of subduing a barbaric murderer.

Wadiya   Well what are *you* going to do?

Naha   My lovemaking will be so intoxicating – he will want his days and nights to be a marathon of pulsating undulating passion, on a sea of me.

Akila   Are you joking? You get out of breath standing up from the toilet.

Naha   There are different kinds of fitness . . . I may not sprint but I have medals for my horizontal jogging. Besides – what's your plan? Use your pen to write away the problems of the world – are you going to write him into submission?

Akila   Well it's working for Scheherazade isn't it?

Fatah   Scheherazade?

Akila   The current wife. She was in here with us until yesterday when she got the call for her 'wedding'.

Fatah   Is she dead?

Akila   Not yet.

Zuya   She'll be fine. Got a battle plan.

Fatah   What plan?

Akila   To tell him stories.

Fatah   Bore him to sleep?

Wadiya   NO – entertain him with such enthralling never-ending stories that he'll keep her alive to hear what comes next.

Fatah   Well, that sounds ok.

Akila   *Ok*? It's *great*

Fatah   As long as . . .

Akila   What?

Fatah   Well – as long as . . .

Zuya   Yes?

Fatah   As long as she's a good storyteller.

Naha   That's a fair point. Is she?

Zuya   I don't know – is she?

Akila   I've got to be honest. She's good at *telling* stories – weaving a yarn – but the *ideas* bit . . . she's not really – the best . . .

Fatah   WE'RE ALL GOING TO DIE!

Zuya   Calm down!

Fatah   LET ME OUT OF HERE, I'M SIXTEEN I HAVE MY WHOLE LIFE AHEAD OF ME!

Naha   Shh! Calm, little one – calm. She can't be that bad. She's lasted one night . . . she's already winning.

Zuya   For now.

Naha *shoots her a look.*

Fatah   What's she like Scheherazade?

Zuya   A warrior – tall and dark [*The actress should use adjectives that describe herself.*]

Wadiya   She moves well – and her hair is long [*The actress should use adjectives that describe herself.*]

Akila   Hard to describe the colour – it's blackish [*The actress should use adjectives that describe herself.*]

Naha   Sometimes close to the candle she's older and you see her lines, sometimes away from the light she's young . . .

Fatah   She sounds like hundreds of other women. Like any woman.

Akila   She is any woman. Every woman. And she is *the* woman. The only one.

Wadiya   The only one for now.

Naha   She's a survivor. She will get through it. I believe.

Fatah (*rising fear*)   But if she doesn't . . .

Naha   if she doesn't – well you'll be alright. look at you, you're so lovely. How could anyone hurt you?

A beat.

Zuya   You know who she reminds me of?

Akila   Scheherazade?

Zuya   No this one. (*Indicating* **Fatah**.) She's very like his first wife

Wadiha   The one who? (*Signifies fucking.*)

With the servant?

Zuya   The one who's the reason we are in this shit in the first place.

Fatah (*terror*)   I don't look like her do I? Then he'll definitely kill me.

Naha   Don't worry – you just need to come up with a back-up plan like Scheherazade.

Akila   What can you do?

Fatah   I make a nice maqloobeh.

Akila   Cooking won't save you now.

Fatah   Then what?

Zuya   Got any good jokes?

Akila   Can you sing?

Fatah *sings (it should be in the Western scale and sound nice and sweet to Western ears)*

> To-morrow is Saint Valentine's day,
> All in the morning betime,
> And I a maid at your window,
> To be your Valentine.
> Then up he rose, and donn'd his clothes,
> And dupp'd the chamber-door;
> Let in the maid, that out a maid
> Never departed more.

Zuya   What the hell was that? You sound like one of them. Occidentals. All throat. No heart or stomach.

She sings a full Arabic scale then morphs into a traditional Arabic love song. Perhaps 'Ataba'.

Naha   That's what the King wants. As well as – you know.

Fatah   This is a nightmare. When I left my house this evening I was excited. All day getting ready – my *teta* and my aunts so attentive – I've never seen so many lotions and potions and smelled so many smells and felt so many feelings. And they whisper things in my ears.

The women gather round her becoming her family.

Zuya (*whispered*)   Don't be afraid.

Naha   We all go through this.

Wadiya   Try and enjoy it.

Akila   Close your eyes.

Zuya   Look right at him.

Naha   Be silent.

Wadiya   Make lots of noise – they like that.

Naha   Act surprised.

Akila   Shy.

Wadiya   But aroused.

Zuya   Even if you aren't.

Wadiya   Touch him.

Naha   Don't touch him.

Akila   Climb on top – they like that.

Zuya   Be in control.

Wadiya   Arch your back.

Akila   Lie flat – like a corpse.

Naha   Don't move a muscle – they like that.

Akila   Follow his lead.

Zuya   Don't show it hurts and

Wadiya   never

Naha   ever

Akila   cry –

Wadiha   they don't like that.

They all step away.

Fatah   And then as if by magic I was at the gates. Of the palace. Dressed like a princess. Shining like a jewel. Smelling like a rose. Waiting to be plucked.

Zuya   You'll be plucked alright.

Akila   We're all plucked.

Fatah   I was ready for anything that could happen. He could be ugly. Or handsome. Beat me. Or stroke me. Eat food off my naked body. Maybe even make me shit on him . . . But of all the things I was expecting – waiting in a room for my inevitable execution was not one of them.

Zuya   It's not inevitable. We must not give up. Scheherazade may not fail.

Akila   Scheherazade *must not* fail. For all our sakes.

Fatah   Well, we better start praying that her stories are good then.

Wadiya   Full of sex

Akila   and suspense

Zuya   and battles

Naha   and intrigue.

Akila   *Is* that what makes a good story? Sex, suspense, battles and intrigue.

Zuya   You tell us, Akila – you're the writer.

Akila   You have to know your audience. What does the King like?

Naha   All those things surely – he's a man.

Wadiya   And dancing.

Akila   They say stories need a beginning, middle and an end, but these stories are different . . . these stories must keep going . . . be threaded very carefully. They must be like a reflection within a reflection within a reflection.

Naha   Why?

Akila   So they go on forever. Keep him guessing. Turning the pages.

Fatah   Like water turning down the plug hole, round and round.

Akila   Exactly, Fatah. That's right. And a good story needs a hook. A hook to catch the attention of a big King Fish. And if we can help Scheherazade to come up with a suitable hook then we ladies we will land that fish and change our destiny – the destiny of all women.

Fatah   How?

Akila   With stories!

Zuya   We'll teach that King a thing or two.

Fatah   Men don't like being taught things. Especially by women.

Akila   They don't need to know they're being taught . . . Never underestimate the power of a good story:

Wadiha   Like the jinni and the fisherman.

Naha   Everyone knows that one.

Akila   Really? Ok then.

She lights a candle and hands it to **Naha** *who starts the story – this is the candle of the* Hakawati *and every time someone tells a story they are given one to signify they are the sun for this moment. So as this story is told the candle is passed from teller to teller.*

Akila   The candle of the storyteller. When you hold it you are the sun. We orbit around you. So. *Yulla*. Tell it. All of us. Together. You start, Naha.

The Women* [*see the note on page 2*]   Ok. So . . . there was a poor fisherman whose family were starving. The less he caught the hungrier they became and the more maggoty his net until one day he was ready to give up. He decided he would put out his net three times and if he hadn't caught some fish by the third he would drown himself and his family.

So praying to himself he goes to the shore and puts out his net for the first time. He feels something heavy and gets excited, so hauls it in – only to find a dead stinking donkey. He curses his luck throws the beast back in and casts his nets a second time.

Hours pass and suddenly he feels something – a tug – he hauls the net in again and finds . . . an old chest . . . It could hold riches aplenty – may hold his future. He fumbles excitedly with the rusty latch and eventually gets it open to discover . . .

Nothing – it was empty. So now the fisherman's fuming. He decides to cast his net one last time. Almost immediately he feels something – not so heavy or big but something in it. When he yanks it in he finds a copper lantern. Dirty but definitely metal – he could sell it at the market and get something to eat. He opens the lantern to see if there's anything inside – no nothing. Then he cleans it on his shirt a little. Suddenly clouds of black smoke fly out of the spout and a jinni appears before him – huge – eyes of fire, a mouth like the opening of hell – the man's so terrified he pisses himself.

The jinni laughs and says, 'You have one wish' – but before the fisherman can get excited the jinni adds, 'Your wish is to choose how you die'. The fisherman is horrified and pleads with the jinni – 'I freed you – surely you should be grateful, not killing me'.

The jinni explains that he had been one of the rebellious jinni that tried to overthrow God. He was sealed in the lantern as punishment and thrown out to sea. He had been trapped for hundreds of years. At first he vowed he would make whoever found him rich beyond his wildest dreams. Then after millennia waiting he got impatient and cross and vowed to vent his fury on whoever released him – killing them instantly.

As the fisherman listened he realised this was one crazy jinni and there was no reasoning with him. He'd need to outfox him. So the fisherman smiles at the jinni – 'You expect me to believe that you – you huge hunk of jinn squeezed into that teeny tiny lamp? I'm not an idiot. This is a trick.'

The jinni insists he has been living there but the fisherman just shakes his head in disbelief. 'Fine,' says the jinni, 'I'll prove it to you' – and just like that he transforms himself into a whisp of smoke and flies back into the lamp which the fisherman corks in a flash.

Wadiha   When the jinni realises he has been tricked he begs and begs the fisherman to release him. But the fisherman says no.

The last line of the story must always be told by **Wadiha** *who blows out the candle to signify the end of the story.*

A beat.

Zuya   We can't just end it there.

Wadiha   Why?

Akila   She's right – it's too finished. Final.

Wadiha   What would you add, oh great writer?

Akila   Well . . . I'd say the fisherman said, 'No, do you think I'm stupid? Don't you know the story of the king and the sage? Let me tell you.'

Fatah   She's wrapped a story in a story – I understand now.

Akila   The jinni didn't know it so the fisherman went on: once there was a king who had a terrible disease – limbs falling off, the works. No one could save him – he tried all the lotions and potions, ointments and pills. Then a sage came and without even touching him cured him. It was a miracle. Everyone was happy and the king showered gifts and blessings on the sage promoting him to high office. But the king's advisor did not like this – he became jealous and warned the king about the sage – if he can cure you without touching you, he could kill you without touching you too – he's a sorcerer and they are dangerous. The king became worried and decided to put the sage to death. The sage begged for his life – much as I begged for my life, the fisherman reminded the jinni, and like you the king ignored the sage's pleas. So the sage said, 'When you have cut my head from my body take this book and turn to page six – if you read the words written there my eyes will open and I will sing to you.'

Naha   That's a bit tame isn't it? A song.

Akila   What would you have him do – open his mouth and suck his cock?

Naha   Good idea – that'd be much more interesting.

Akila   Fine. The sage said, 'When you have cut my head from my body take this book and turn to page six – if you read the words written there my mouth will open and I will suck your cock'. The king was delighted –

Naha   You bet he was.

Akila   So he took the book and called the executioner who removed the sage's head from his body. Next the king excitedly turned to page six of the book ready to read the incantation and receive his cock sucking – but there was nothing written there – he licked his finger to break up the stiff pages and turned them over – there was nothing written in the book at all. The king was confused but before an answer to this riddle could form he dropped down dead. The sage had poisoned the pages. 'So you see, jinni,' said the fisherman, 'if you had let me live I would have let you live but you would surely have killed me so I must do away with you.'

Fatah   Then what happens?

Naha   How about he pleasures himself?

Akila   You're obsessed.

Wadiha   He has to free him –

Akila   Yes – so the jinni begs and promises the fisherman to bewitch his net so the fish jump into it.

Naha   Great, so he lets him out of the lamp

Zuya   and the jinni strikes him dead.

Akila   *No* – we want to show people in power can learn – change. That's the moral. He doesn't kill him.

Naha   he takes him to a spot high up and tells him to cast his nets.

Akila   That's right and they immediately fill with fish. And the fisherman worries he will have to waste them – he could never sell so many.

Fatah   But then they turn into beautiful jewels and diamonds – sparkling,

Zuya   and the fisherman is rich and happy and the jinni flies off into another story. Perfect!

Fatah   But how do we link it?

Zuya   Let Scheherazade figure it out – she's gotta do *something*, we can't do it all.

Naha   How about it ends saying, 'The fisherman was lucky but not as lucky as his brother the porter . . .'

Akila   That's a great hook . . . I'll write those down – you all come up with ideas for the porter's story . . .

They take pens and paper and begin to write, except **Naha** *who goes to each corner of the room and spits, chanting* 'baraka, baraka, baraka' *as she does.*

Zuya   What is she doing?

Akila   Cleansing the room from the jinn.

Zuya   *Majnouna!*

Naha   DON'T call me mad – you should be thanking me for saving you all from the bad spirits.

She continues her task.

Fatah   Hold on – how are we going to get these stories to her? To Scheherazade?

A knowing look between **Akila** *and* **Wadiha**.

Akila   Just write, little one. Come on – write . . . ALL OF YOU!

They set to action.

Akila We need lots of stories. Lots and lots. Don't worry how we get the stories to her – just hope that he likes them – pray she tells them well – that she lasts another night . . . or it'll be us next . . .

They all set to writing ferociously as though their lives depend on it, as it does. Music signifies the passing of time. Perhaps there is a tally on the wall or the floor with chalk to denote how many nights have passed.

Five Nights

Naha I'm tired.

Zuya You're always tired.

Akila Think about Scheherazade – think about how tired she must be. Telling him stories all night long, then all day coming up with new ones . . . well, reading ours and learning them . . .

Naha She's not just telling stories either . . .

Fatah What's he like. The King?

Akila What do you think he's like?

Fatah Oh I don't know . . .

Zuya Tall.

Naha Dark.

Wadiha Handsome.

Akila Like all Arab men.

Zuya Or Hairy.

Wadiha Spitty.

Naha Plotting.

Zuya   Evil.

Wadiha   Religious.

Akila   Like all Arab men.

Fatah   I prefer the first version.

Akila   Fine, stick with that.

Fatah   But I want to know what he's really like. What will it *be* like with him. Will I like it?

Zuya   *If* you end up in his bedroom and *if* you end up in his bed, under his weight all you'll be thinking about is the fact that desert is your red, red blood splashed all over the room.

Fatah *runs to the door in fear trying to open it but it is locked fast.*

Fatah   I. NEED. MY. BLOOD. I. WANT. TO. LIVE.

Naha *goes to her and stops her.*

Naha   Then put your imagination into something useful, *ya binti*. Put it into a story. You haven't shared even one yet.

Fatah   I have got one – I just don't want to /

Akila *gets a candle – lights it and hands it to her.*

Akila   *Yulla*, don't be shy.

Fatah   But what if it's not good enough?

Zuya   Be brave. The writer has to be fearless – the *Hakawati* is a warrior – *yulla*.

Fatah *slowly, fearfully takes a deep breath and haltingly begins, but grows in confidence.*

Fatah   There once was a very poor farmer who lived in a small house with his wife. They had one dunum at the back to grow vegetables and a small yard at the front with a lemon tree on either side.

Now the farmer worked hard, as most do, getting up early and working till dusk. Every night he was so tired that as soon as his head hit the pillow he fell into a deep sleep. That is until one night when he has a strange dream. He describes it to his wife the next morning: 'In my dream,' he says, 'I had to go to Damascus Gate in Jerusalem – I didn't know why, just that something would happen there that was vitally important.' 'How strange,' says the wife, and the two think nothing more of it and go on with their day. But the next night the farmer has the same dream, and the night after, and the night after that, until his wife tells him that this is obviously a sign – he should go to the gate, and see what happens.

So the next day he packs some bread, za'atar and water and trudges the long road to Jerusalem. It takes him two whole days to get there, and when he does he goes and waits by the gate. He waits and waits all day but nothing happens. So he goes and finds somewhere to sleep for the night under a tree, and the next day he goes back to his spot by the gate, again nothing happens that day. On the third day when he takes up post once more he's approached by a shopkeeper from across the road. The woman says to him: 'I've been watching you these three days just stood here by the gate – do you mind me asking you what you are doing – I'm curious.' The farmer tells the shopkeeper his story and at the end the woman is laughing loudly at him. 'You are a stupid man,' she says. 'You've wasted three working days to come here and do nothing; that'll teach you to follow your dreams. Where would we be if we all did that – for example, I keep having a dream about treasure buried in the yard of a house between two lemon trees.' Before the woman had finished speaking the farmer had scurried away leaving the shopkeeper puzzled and scratching her head. 'What a strange man,' she thought.

A beat – **Fatah** *blows out the candle.*

Fatah   I'd love to see Al-Quds – Damascus Gate . . . I've never even left this city . . . (*A beat.*) My *teta* used to tell me that story.

Wadiha   It means follow your dreams . . .

Fatah   If only I was allowed to go there.

Akila   Shhh, don't spoil the mood . . . the afterglow of the story – it's nice.

Naha   What is this – nursery time?

Akila   Respect the *Hakawati*.

Naha   I thought we were going to excite, arouse, so far it's all been Mother bloody Goose. They're sweet stories and everything but don't you think we need something a bit more. You know. X-rated.

Wadiha   Go on then – what's your brilliant X-rated story, oh, great *Hakawati*?

Naha   I can't just pull one out of my ass.

Wadiha   Then don't be a critic. If you don't write the stories you don't get to criticise.

Akila   It doesn't work like that. Everyone has an opinion. Whether you want it or not. And the problem with telling stories is every *hmar* thinks he can do it. Did I ask for their opinion? *No*. Do they share it with me? Of course.

A beat while she fumes.

Naha   Well, now there's only one person whose opinion matters. THE KING. And, Wadiha – I think *you* have a story for him don't you

Wadiha   Well . . .

Naha   Oh, you do – one that will tickle his turban and caress his kaftan . . .

Akila *hands her a lit candle, but* **Wadiha** *looks stubbornly at* **Naha**.

Wadiha   I don't know if I'm ready to tell it. Out loud.

Akila   Then I will tell it for you –

She indicates for **Wadiha** *to give her the paper she has written the story on and takes the candle, then reads it out loud.*** [See the note on page 2]**

Ok, so gather near, my sisters, and let me tell you the truth about love and desire. This is about a woman. She loved a young man who loved her back since they were teenagers. Their love for each other was strong like a ball of steel. No matter how much you hit or threw the ball, it remained unchanged. They married and spent their honeymoon eating lamb and duck and pouncing on each other until they fell asleep. They were stuck together like an orange and its navel. She was the soil that wants to be watered and watered and he was like the waterfall wanting to gush and gush without pause.

Naha   Gushing. Wonderful.

Akila (*reading*)   Days and months were spent like this, with both living in a perpetual honeymoon. But the seas were calling him and he obeyed. Her ambitious husband rode the boats that traversed the seas. Trading, selling, negotiating, returning laden with coins and jewels that he would spread beneath her feet. She would show gratitude for his gifts even though all she wanted to do was to take him in her arms and banish the loneliness she felt during his absence.

One day when he was travelling she woke up with a lot of energy and headed to the market. She smiled at the sun and everything around her, even the blond youth who, as soon as her smile reached him, started following her from alley to alley and shop to shop. Every time she turned, he was behind her.

Her heart fluttered and sang as she entered a women-only bathhouse and the steam of the hot water whispered in her pores 'you long for a man, you long for a man'. When she left, the young man was waiting for her, and he followed her home. She opened the door and left it open. The youth entered and every part of him was pleading and begging: his eyes, mouth, arms, abdomen, thighs. So she let her body taste the forbidden wine of his lips instead of the vinegar that had settled in her soul during her husband's absence. She became infatuated with the youth so much that when her husband returned from his travels she wished the waves had overwhelmed his boat and drowned him. She began to count the seconds until his next trip.

Then a messenger arrived inviting her husband to a dinner at the house of Sindbad. Her heart danced and swayed with happiness because while he was gone she could meet the blond youth.

She said she would accompany her husband in order to see Sindbad's famous palace from outside. In reality she wanted to make sure he was safely inside the palace so she could hurry to her blond youth and dissolve in his arms without worry.

Outside, one of the palace guards approached her and asked if she wanted to go in. She thanked him, following her husband with her eyes as he walked through the palace's orchard, and when he disappeared from sight she turned and flew like a butterfly. Running away from the guard, to her house where she saw the blond boy waiting for her, weeping. Indoors together she in turn cried until their bodies began to converse with frantic breaths and kisses.

But a knock at the door terrified them. 'My husband must have come back!' In the blink of an eye she hid the youth in the basement. Then she opened the door only to find the palace guard in front of her. He leapt on her as if she was freshly made dough and he was the oven giving her heat. She swelled and rose with desire and forgot about the entire world. They both let out mighty screams as they climaxed. His was like the roar of a lion and hers the song of a blackbird. But now yet another knock on the door.

It was her husband. Her heart skipped a beat but her mind became alert. She whispered to the guard to shout and threaten-to throw her in jail. The guard didn't understand but when the woman knelt down and tossed her hair and began wailing, he did as she had told him. He shouted and insulted her loudly, making sure her husband heard all this. Then, when he entered, the guard put his sword back in his scabbard and left quickly, full of fake anger.

The husband rushed to his wife and helped her up asking 'What happened?' as he hugged her to him. She told him how she was feeding the hungry cats outside the house as usual, when a young man appeared begging her for help. 'There is a palace guard who falsely accuses me of stealing. He wants to take me to prison.' She felt sorry for the youth and hid him in the basement, 'But the guard kicked down the door, took out his sword and questioned me about the boy. I said he wasn't here, but the guard threatened and insulted me. Until you came to save me.'

Her husband held her to him praising her bravery and valour. Then he hurried to the basement and released the youth who flew out of the house like a fiery arrow.

The woman was so relieved and overjoyed her lungs clapped like two hands after holding her breath for so long. What happened was truly a miracle. First, she saved herself. Second, she is still married and her husband loves her. Third, she succeeded in getting rid of the youth without him realising that the guard broke into her house and her heart.

Naha   And her knickers.

Zuya   Shush, Naha!

Akila   This, my sisters is the story of the woman, as she told it to me word by word. She begged me not to file her story under the category of womanly deceit because desire is not deceitful. Desire and love go hand in hand.

She said: 'I saved myself from the vengeance of my husband who, if he had known the truth, would have killed me. And I saved the youth from my husband. And I saved my husband from the sword of the palace guard. And I saved the guard from scandal. And in so doing I saved myself from deprivation and longing.'

Akila *blows out the candle.*

Fatah   It's beautiful

Akila   Erotic

Naha   She's a goer!

Akila   It's clever – the way it excuses her behaviour in the end.

A beat.

Zuya   It's a bit. I dunno – read out.

Wadiha   Because she read it out.

Akila   Literary, you mean it's a bit literary.

Fatah   But it's still sexy.

Naha   I got wet with all that rising dough and ovens talk.

Fatah   NAHA!

Naha   What? It's true.

Akila   But remember Scheherazade's not reading it – she's acting. Writer-performer. She will improvise a bit.

Fatah   She won't learn it by heart – say it the way Wadiha wrote it?

Naha   She'll tell the story but it won't be exactly the same.

Fatah   But in *my* story about Damascus Gate it's my words. I don't want her to paraphrase. I put them in that order for a reason . . .

Akila   You can't be so precious, little writer. Actors make the writing better.

Zuya   Only if they're good.

Fatah   What if they're not good?

Akila   Well, Scheherazade can't be too bad, she's keeping him entertained

Naha   For now.

A beat.

Zuya   I don't believe it. That story. All the affairs. That woman. It doesn't ring true.

Naha *and* **Wadiha** *share a look.*

Akila   Does that matter? Why does it have to be true?

Zuya   It doesn't, but we have to *believe* it's possible otherwise what's the point.

Naha   And you didn't believe it?

Zuya   Not really – and I'd like it more if I did.

Wadiha   Believe it. It's true. All of it.

Zuya   No way.

Wadiha   I know. (*A beat.*) It's my story.

Zuya   What?! Then what happened to your husband?

Wadiha   Drowned.

The women all seem surprised.

Fatah   And that guard in the story? Is *he* one of the ones [guarding us] –

Wadiha   Don't be silly . . .

Akila   But she does have a way with men in uniform . . .

Fatah   So that's how we are getting the stories to Scheherazade! One of the guards!

A beat.

Zuya   But what if he goes off you?

Wadiha   He won't.

Zuya   Or changes his mind?

Wadiha/Naha   He won't.

Zuya   Or gets found out and executed?

Akila   We have to hope he won't. Because if Scheherazade stops getting stories it's over for all of us.

A beat.

Zuya   So you're telling me we are relying on a fucking man?!

Naha   We don't have any choice – any control over that.

Akila   But this – this we do – so come on – write!

She hands her writing implements – time passes. Music may signify this.

Fifty Nights

The women are all writing. **Fatah** *suddenly tears up the paper she's writing on.*

Zuya   What is it?

Fatah   Rubbish – it's all rubbish. I don't want to do this anymore. I want to go home

She jumps up and rushes to the door trying to open it and get out.

Fatah   I can't breathe! I want air – light – I need to get out of this this this – coffin! LET ME OUT! LET ME OUT! LET ME OUT! LET ME OUT! LET ME OUT!

Zuya *goes to her and puts her hand over her mouth.*

Zuya   Shhh.

Wadiha   We mustn't annoy them.

Naha   Be good girls.

Akila   Do as we're told.

Zuya   Not kick.

Wadiha   Scratch.

Akila   Punch.

Zuya   Bite.

Naha   Lie still.

Akila   Pretend that we are already dead.

Wadiha   They like that.

Fatah   Why? WHY DO THEY LIKE THAT? We're alive
. . . WE'RE STILL ALIVE IN HERE.

She rushes from **Zuya** *and the others and bangs on the door; the
others try to stop her, then suddenly a banging comes in response. It is
the noise of a hundred swords bashing on the outside of the room in
which the women are trapped. It is loud – overpowering,
threatening, terrifying.*

Fatah *screams,* **Naha** *holds her – they all huddle together in fear
until the noise abates.*

Fatah (*quietly*)   They'll forget about us and we will die. That
– that woman won't remind anyone we are here – she needs
us – needs our stories and we will be stuck here forever.

Naha   No, no, little one, don't let your mind go there.
That's a bad place.

Akila   What we need is a good story – cheer us up. Come
on, Zuya. A strong story – about winning . . .

Zuya   I have one – about a fox but – no, it's not quite right for now . . .

Akila   Wadiha?

Wadiha *shakes her head*

Naha   Ok, ok . . . *Mashi*. I have a good story. Something cheeky to take us away, so . . .

Akila *hands her a lit candle as she begins to talk. In* **Naha***'s story the women should take on some of the speaking roles to dramatise it.*

Naha   This happened in a hammam in a small village outside of Fustat, so far away from here but, *wallah*, I have good sources that every word is true.

I heard it from my cousin Esraa, who heard from Um Mohammed, who heard it from Nour, Salah Nasrallah's daughter, who heard it from Um Soliman, who swore that she heard it from Um Hakim, who heard it from her daughter's friend, the hammam masseuse herself, so it must be true.

Zuya   Just get on with it.

Naha   Ok, so . . . *Marra*, there was this woman, Safiya, she was the local butcher's wife. *Khalas*, she was at the age where her children were grown and married themselves, and her wedding bed was a bit . . . cold. Safiya was a woman of pride and always managed to get what she wanted, except for her husband's attention. It had been years since she felt that man's touch. She tried everything to seduce him, putting her hair up and lining her eyes, wearing revealing clothes to bed, a couples of times she even climbed on top of him only to find him fast asleep. It was useless. And so she gave up and accepted the life God had provided her.

But then . . .

One Thursday she goes to the hammam as usual, to bathe and clean her hair and relax. She arrives, she washes herself and then decides to get a massage. She calls the girl over and the girl starts to massage her. She starts with the shoulders, and works her way down. After a few minutes Safiya is passed out, completely asleep. The girl tries to wake her but it's useless so she leaves.

Hours later, they're getting ready to close the hammam, almost no one is left. Safiya begins to feel something . . . down there. She wakes up to see this head in between her thighs, and she's wondering who could it be. She sits up against the edge to check that no one is there and closes her eyes, pressing herself against the head. Urging it on. Safiya has been waiting for this, waiting for this sensation, waiting for this hotness, for . . . this moment . . . and FINALLY! She does everything in her power not to scream too loud and collapses back on the floor.

BOOM! As she hits the ground – CRACK! – she feels something break under her.

She quickly recovers.

Stands up.

Looks down at the floor.

And . . .

It's a puppy! She had fallen on to the puppy that had given her the most intense pleasure she's ever felt, crushed it. Snapped its neck.

Safiya   Oh no!

Naha   Safiya then notices the tag.

Safiya   Yeeeeeeh, it's the king's puppy! *Ya lahwiiii*! He's going to kill me! Safiya, what did you do? *Keda*, you get yourself killed for an orgasm? What am I going to do? *Wallah*, you deserve to die, *ya* Safiya, you fool!

Naha   At this point Um Hassanein, the owner of the hammam, comes in to tell Safiya that it's time to leave.

Um Hassanein   Closing time! *Yalla*, finish up, it's time to leave, I don't care if there's still soap in your – oh dear God above! What's this? Why is there a dead dog in here?

Safiya   You're asking me? What kind of establishment are you running here? Letting in dogs . . . letting – letting people drag dead dogs in – I want my money back!

Um Hassanein   How do I know this is not your dog?

Safiya   My d – Well . . . I . . . Um Hassanein, you know I don't own a dog!

Um Hassanein   How do I know you didn't sneak one in anyway?

Safiya   Because . . . It's the king's dog.

Um Hassanein   THE KING'S DOG?

Safiya   Yes.

Um Hassanein   Safiya! Did you kill the king's puppy?

Safiya   I . . . Well . . . Yes.

Um Hassanein   Safiya!

Safiya   I didn't mean to! I – it just happened.

Um Hassanein   Why are you killing puppies in my hammam?!

Safiya   I didn't kill – it was by mistake!

Um Hassanein   How? How did it happen?

Safiya   I fell. You know how I told you that the steps here are too slippery, well, I slipped and fell on top of it.

Um Hassanein   He's going to kill you.

Safiya   It's your hammam, he's going to kill us both.

Naha   The women then take a moment to look at each other, thinking about the time someone picked flowers from the royal garden without permission. It did not end well.

Safiya You need to help me, Um Hassanein, there must be a way to fix this.

Um Hassanein Ok, come with me, I think I know a jinni that can help us.

Safiya Um Hassanein . . . remember last time?

Um Hassanein Don't worry, my dear, this is a different one, this one lives in the sewers.

Safiya The sewers?

Um Hassanein Trust me.

Naha So the women head towards the sewers to the jinni. They arrive at a hole in the ground, and Um Hassanein pulls the cover away and yells.

Um Hassanein JINNI! MAY YOU HELP ME OVER THE EARTH AND MAY IT BRING YOU PEACE UNDER IT!

Naha They wait for a bit. When they don't receive a response, Um Hassanein tries again.

Um Hassanein JINNI! JINNI! ARE YOU DEAF? I SAID MAY YOU HELP ME OVER THE EARTH –

Jinni OK! OK! I HEARD YOU THE FIRST TIME. I'M COMING!

Um Hassanein What's his problem?

Naha And out of the hole the jinni appears. Unlike the jinni of the lamp or the fields, this jinni looks fragile and old. He moves slowly and has a large frown amidst a million wrinkles on his face. He reaches the top, he looks at the women then glances at the bag containing the puppy. He raises his frown slightly.

Jinni How may I help you women?

Naha Um Hassanein pushes Safiya forward.

Safiya   We . . . I mean . . . I – we were wondering if you could help us?

Jinni   Yes . . . Help you with what?

Safiya   You see . . . We were in the hammam . . . And I was just having a massage, which is something I like to do before I clean my –

Um Hassanein   Safiya killed the king's puppy.

Safiya   I didn't kill it! I fell on it.

Jinni   What kind of person kills a puppy?

Safiya   It was an accident!

Jinni   What do you want me to do about it?

Um Hassanein   Fix it.

Jinni   Fix what exactly?

Um Hassanein   I don't know! The puppy, the situation, something has to be fixed. Make sure I don't lose my business and Safiya here doesn't lose her head.

Jinni   Hmm . . . This looks like it's going to be a hassle.

Um Hassanein   Pff . . . Come on, jinni, what do you want in exchange for this favour?

Naha   The jinni thinks for a moment, then looks at the women and says:

Jinni   Ok, I can help you. If you suck my cock.

Um Hassanein   Eeeehhhh!

Wadiha   What is it with you and cock sucking?

Naha (*continuing regardless*)   Um Hassanein smacks the jinni on the back of head.

Um Hassanein   *Fi eih*? What's wrong with you? Give us something realistic to do! Suck your cock, *eih*? What cock? Is this a joke?

Jinni   Alright, alright, woman! No need for all this. It was worth a try.

Um Hassanein   Worth a try? I'll tell you what's worth a try –

Safiya   Um Hassanein!

Um Hassanein   The things I have to deal with! At my age! Allah, what have I done to deserve this? *Ya rab*, give me the strength –

Safiya   Um Hassanein, please!

Jinni   Yes control yourself, woman!

Um Hassanein   What did you say to me you dirty old –

Safiya   Please! We don't have time for this.

Jinni   Listen to your friend, do you want my help or not?

Um Hassanein   . . . Fine. I'm done. For now.

Safiya   Ok, jinni, tell us.

Jinni   Alright. So. I will help you, in exchange though I want a moment from you.

Um Hassanein   What?

Safiya   You want . . .

Jinni   A moment. I want a moment from you.

Um Hassanein   Jinni, no funny business.

Jinni   I'm being serious. *Yaani*, I ask you to suck my cock, you say no, I ask for a moment, you tell me no funny business. *Wallahi*, I should leave you both to die. He's going to turn you into dog food and feed you to his new puppy, I've been here a long time, I know how this man thinks. Mark my words –

Safiya   Ok! *Khalas!* You'll have a moment, whatever that means. Now tell us what to do.

Jinni   I can make a new puppy. In order to do this, I need you to bring me three things. Energy, warmth and curiosity.

Safiya   Energy, warmth and curiosity.

Jinni   Yes.

Safiya   How are we supposed to do that?

Jinni   You know how this goes, I've told you what I need, it's up to you to find it.

Naha   The women look at each other. How are they supposed to bring energy, warmth and curiosity? It made little sense, and it's not like that they had a lot of time to think about it either! It was only a few hours before sunset.

And so feeling a bit discouraged, and very confused, they set off.

As they were walking through the village, each deep in thought, a man stopped them for directions. He was carrying a big bag on his back. He was wearing a foreign hat and several objects around his neck.

Explorer   I'm sorry, I'm looking for somewhere to eat and sleep?

Naha   Safiya started to answer his question:

Safiya   There's an inn –

Naha   But Um Hassanein sniffed an opportunity . . .

Um Hassanein   Where are you from?

Explorer   Oh, I am an explorer, I've come from the east. I've been travelling for so long, I've forgotten where I have begun this journey.

Um Hassanein   So why do you keep moving?

Explorer   There is so much to see in the world! I can't stop until I have seen every bit of it, tasted every food, drunk from every river.

Um Hassanein   That's very nice. How do you know where to go?

Explorer   I don't.

Um Hassanein   And you've crossed the desert without knowing where you're going??

Explorer   Haha, no I use this bit of technology.

Naha   He points to one of the objects around his neck.

Explorer   This is a compass, it helps me orient myself and thus I can keep discovering new places, new people –

Um Hassanein   Very interesting. The inn is around the corner from here, come we'll walk you.

Naha   The women begin to walk with the foreigner. Safiya senses that something is up and whispers:

Safiya   Um Hassanein, what are you doing?

Um Hassanein   That compiss. We need that.

Safiya   What?

Um Hassanein   Curiosity. That's curiosity, how else would a foreigner end up in this part of the world?

Safiya   You want to borrow the man's compass?

Um Hassanein   Borrow, take, something like that.

Safiya   Um Hassanein!

Um Hassanein   Shh!

Safiya   If we take it then the man will be lost!

Um Hassanein   And if we don't then we'll be dead!

Safiya   But he needs it to travel.

Um Hassanein   He can just stay here, might do him good to stay put for a bit.

Safiya   He's an explorer! He'll be out in the desert by tomorrow, how will be find his way?

Um Hassanein   Let him use the stars, the old-fashioned way.

Naha   At this point they arrive at the inn. The say goodbye to the man, but wait outside.

Um Hassanein   Do you see him?

Safiya   He's having dinner now.

Um Hassanein   Is he wearing the compiss?

Safiya   No.

Um Hassanein   Ok, let's go!

Naha   Quickly they climb through his room's window, grab the man's compass and continue their walk. As they are walking, full of excitement at finding something to take to the jinni, Safiya suddenly trips.

Safiya   Hey!

Naha   It's a man sleeping in the road.

Safiya   Sorry! I didn't see you there!

Man   Watch where you're going, woman!

Um Hassanein   Ok, she said sorry! Why are you sleeping in the middle of the road, why don't you go sleep in a chicken coop like everyone usually does? Stupid people.

Naha   As Um Hassanein shouted at this man, she notices that he was sleeping under a blanket which is why they didn't notice him to begin with. Immediately she gets an idea.

Um Hassanein   Safiya! The blanket.

Safiya   What?

Um Hassanein   His blanket! Warmth!

Safiya   Um Hassanein, what is wrong with you? This man has no home.

Um Hassanein   How do you know that? He looks like Ali ibn Bakr's son, he's probably been kicked out.

Safiya   The blanket keeps him warm!

Um Hassanein   Who needs warmth in this weather?

Safiya   He's sleeping in the street!

Um Hassanein   He shouldn't be upsetting his father then.

Safiya   We don't even know if it's Ali.

Um Hassanein   *Yalla*, he's going back to sleep, not even using the blanket properly, he won't notice it's gone I promise you.

Naha   Um Hassanein sneaks up behind the man who had already fallen fast asleep, only half covered. She grabs the edge of the blanket and slowly pulls it off him. The man stirs but doesn't wake up.

Um Hassanein   Let's go before he wakes up again!

Naha   And they walk off quickly.

Safiya   You're going to hell and you're taking me with you.

Um Hassanein   *Estakhfarallah*! Why are you being so dramatic, Safiya? I'll bring him a new blanket tomorrow, I'll even go chat to his father.

Safiya   You don't know it's Ali!

Um Hassanein   It might as well be. Like his father would know the difference!

Safiya   We're stealing now. Stealing!

Naha   As they stood there arguing, suddenly a boy runs between them screaming in joy, holding a kite. He lets go and the kite flies in the air. The boy continues running, looking up, eyes sparkling with excitement.

Without even thinking about it, **Safiya** *then grabs the kite's string and snaps it.*

Safiya   RUN!

Naha   Before the boy could even process what happened, the women run back towards the jinni's sewer holding the compass, the blanket and the flying kite.

They arrive a few minutes before sunset.

Um Hassanein   JINNI! WE'RE HERE! JINNI, WE GOT THE THREE THINGS!

JINNI, WHERE ARE YOU? YOU HELP ME OVER THE EARTH –

Jinni   ALRIGHT! STOP SHOUTING! YOU DON'T HAVE TO SAY THAT EVERY TIME!

Um Hassanein   But isn't that the way to summon you?

Jinni   I prefer not to use the term 'summon'.

Um Hassanein   So what 'term' do you use?

Jinni   I prefer –

Safiya   It doesn't matter! We're here, we have the three things.

Um Hassanein   Warmth.

Naha   Um Hassanein hands over the blanket.

Um Hassanein   Curiosity.

Naha   She hands over the compass.

Safiya   And energy.

Naha   Safiya hands over the kite.

The jinni looks at the objects. The women can't tell if he looks impressed or disgusted under all those wrinkles.

Jinni   Very well. Give me a minute.

Naha The jinni then disappears into the sewer. A couple of minutes pass and he emerges holding a tiny, fluffy bundle.

Jinni Have a look, does it look like the one you killed?

Safiya Jinni! What's this? His mouth is huge! Have you ever seen a puppy with teeth bigger than its paws?

Jinni You're right. I thought it looked a bit strange. One second, I'll be right back.

Naha The jinni disappears for a minute. By now the sun has set and the guards can be heard looking for the puppy. The jinni appears again.

Jinni What about now?

Naha Safiya looks at the dog, and relief floods her.

Safiya Yes! It's identical! Oh, jinni, thank you!

Um Hassanein *Alhamdulillah*! Thank you, God, for getting us out of this mess!

Jinni I got you out of this mess.

Um Hassanein Yes! Thank you, jinni, for not being full of shit.

Jinni I can keep this puppy you know? I've always wanted –

Um Hassanein No! Sorry, jinni. Thank you, thank you for everything, thank you for saving us, thank you for being so gracious, so kind, thank you for your wisdom, without you we would not be here right now, without you –

Jinni Yes, yes, now it's time for you to pay me back.

Um Hassanein Yes, of course, anything!

Safiya Except for . . . well, you know.

Jinni We had a deal. I want a moment from you.

Safiya Yes, yes. How do I give you a moment?

Jinni   You humans always find ways to connect, even for just a moment. That's all I ask for, I want you to give me one of those moments.

Naha   The women look at one another, they're both at a loss at what to do. The guards' calls are getting louder. Safiya thinks about the moments she's had that have stayed with her, the day her daughter smiled for the first time, the gifts a boy used to leave by her window, the time she swam in the Nile in the middle of the night, the first time she heard a song sung by her grandmother . . . (**Safiya** *begins to hum a tune.*)

Naha   That's it, she thought. I can give him that moment. And so Safiya stood in front of the jinni and sang him the song, a lullaby. (*The humming becomes singing.*) She couldn't remember the words perfectly, she wasn't entirely sure of the melody, but the more she sang, the stronger the memory became and the memory filled her, and filled that space between her and the jinni. Soon she forgot that this was a deal, that it wasn't her grandmother singing, that it was her voice. At the end of the song, the jinni thanked her, handed the puppy to her and quietly went back into his sewer.

Um Hassanein   Well done, Safiya. I really thought we were done for.

Safiya   *Yalla*, let's go home. It's been a long day.

Naha   And so the women start to head home in silence. Um Hassanein's mind full of thoughts about how she needed to cleanse her hammam from bad spirits – she was going to need to strike a bargain though, because the local exorcist is always trying to rip people off.

Um Hassanein   The bastard!

Naha   And Safiya's mind, trying to push out those gnawing thoughts, those quiet thoughts that the puppy maybe didn't look quite as identical as she thought, something deep inside is telling her there was something about the eyes, maybe it

was the light but it looked like maybe, just maybe, this dog
had one blue eye and one green . . . No, she must have
imagined it . . .

A beat – she blows out the candle.

Naha   Now that's a story . . .

Fatah   The dog – licked her – is that even –?

Wadiha   I liked it.

Zuya   Me too.

Fatah   And the jinni was so – ergh.

Naha   It made you forget though didn't it?

Akila   For those few minutes you forgot you were stuck in
here. You were transported. All your worries gone.

Fatah   It's true.

Naha   So let's keep magicking ladies. It's our only hope.
The only way out of here. Ok, beauty? No more attempted
escapes, ah? We need to keep the guards on side.

Fatah *nods but still looks longingly at the doors.*

Zuya *starts spitting in the corners of the room chanting* 'baraka,
baraka, baraka'.

Naha   I thought you didn't believe in that.

Zuya   It can't hurt. Besides it's a better way to cleanse the
place than my bitch of a mother's.

Akila   What did she do?

Zuya   Spray us all with her piss.

Fatah   Did it work?

Zuya   I'm in here aren't I? But we need all the help we can
get . . .

Naha *gives her a look.*

Zuya (*to* **Naha**)   We don't have an endless supply of stories do we? And when we run out . . .

Naha *gives her a look indicating* **Fatah** – *she doesn't want her upset again.* **Zuya** *resumes her task. The others all set to writing. Music signifies the passing of time. Perhaps there is a tally on the wall or the floor with chalk to denote how many nights have passed.*

One Hundred Nights

The women have all drifted off while working. **Wadiya** *is gone. Suddenly* **Naha** *wakes up.*

Naha   She's gone! Wake up – wake up everyone – we're doomed – Scheherazade has failed.

Zuya   How do you know?

Naha   Wadiha has gone. She was next.

Naha *wails, crying out in fear in Arabic she wasn't expecting this, she can't keep up a brave face –* **Fatah** *runs to comfort her, shocked at this reaction.*

Fatah   Don't worry about Wadiha – her dancing will entrance him. For now.

Naha   But what if it doesn't?

Zuya   Then I'll go next and kill the bastard.

Akila   You're all talk. You've never killed a man.

Zuya   Why was I in prison then?

Akila   You were in prison?

Zuya   You're surprised?

Akila   Not really.

Fatah   What happened?

Zuya   I don't tell that story.

Akila   Scheherazade has failed. The great *Hakawati* has overstretched herself – we are all going to die because she thought she was better than she is.

Zuya   Silly bitch – she gave us all false hope but deep down I knew she was useless – a waste of time – lazy – self-centred – vain – nothing special.

Naha   A false goddess

Zuya   like the useless fucking *asfoura*.

Fatah   Sparrow?

Zuya   It's a stupid story my lying cow of a mother used to tell me.

Akila   Tell it – it might calm us.

Zuya   I don't want to.

Akila   Tell it.

Zuya   NO!

All   TELL IT!

Fatah   We need it . . . please . . .

Akila *hands her the candle.*

Zuya   OH FINE! There was once a sparrow who thought very highly of himself – he thought his pathetic tweets were the dulcet tones of a nightingale – that his dunn feathers could outshine a peacock. He didn't realise what a dull, scrawny pathetic useless thing he was. One day he witnessed something astonishing as he was perched on the branch of a tree near some grazing sheep – an eagle suddenly flew down and grabbed one of the animals with her tallons and flew off with it. The sparrow was beside himself – what a feat! What a meal! How bold and outrageous! What daring!

He was also very turned on. He decided he wanted this amazing eagle for himself. For his wife. So he started following her around places. Watching her every move. And at last he found her nest. He waited til nightfall when she was asleep and then he flew down to try and make love to her. The eagle felt a strange movement in the nest and cocked an eye to see what was happening. And there was this little sparrow jiggling about.

'What are you doing?' she asked. 'Seducing you,' said the sparrow. 'Seducing me? I'm the queen of the birds and you are a scrawny little worm-eating embarrassment. Get lost before I crush you with my beak and feed you to my chicks.'

The sparrow was miffed. I'll show that eagle, he thought. I'll bring her a delicious sheep for her dinner, then she'll see my worth. Then she'll want me.

So the next day the stupid sparrow headed to try and catch a sheep for the eagle's dinner. He flew up high over the flock as he'd seen her do, and chose the largest animal he could spot, then flew down, his little feet outstretched to grab it. Of course he'd gone for the biggest beast of all – the ram whose coat was matted and dirty and his little sparrow feet got tangled so not only could he not lift the thing he was now enmeshed – trapped and unable to fly away. The shepherd witnessed all this and was bemused. He went to the sparrow and freed it only to place it in a cage and give it as a gift to his daughter. And that was it for the sparrow. Trapped in a cage of his own making because of his arrogance and lack of humility.

She blows out the candle.

Fatah   Your *mother* told you that story?

Zuya   Yup. To stop me going to school. Bitch. She said deep down she knew I was useless – a waste of time – lazy – self-centred –nothing special . . . but she didn't give me a chance to be anything. She'd already made up her mind . . .

Fatah   How could she be so cruel?

Zuya   I reminded her of my father . . .

There is a round of applause from **Wadiha** *who has returned and been listening to all this. She carries a tray of fruit and a letter.*

Fatah   You're back!

Akila   What happened?

Zuya   We thought he had carved you up.

Naha   That Scheherazade had overstretched herself . . .

Wadiha   So did I. While you were all asleep one of the guards – not mine – he woke me and led me out of the room. I thought my time had come. That the sickle blade of death was hanging over my head. I was ready to do my final dance.

She starts to sway and move. Music rises. We think she is going to dance to an Arabic song. Anticipation builds – she sways more – but then she stops as suddenly as the music does.

Wadiha   But no. The guard was calling to give me these.

She signifies what she is holding.

Fatah   What is it?

Wadiha   A platter – and a letter.

Zuya   Who from?

Wadiha   The woman herself.

Fatah   Scheherazade?

Akila   What does it say?

Naha   Probably a thank you.

Wadiha   See for yourself.

She hands the note to **Akila**. *The other women gather round and read over her shoulder. They are incredulous.*

Fatah   I can't – believe it –

Akila   Of all the nerve.

Naha   Cheek. That's what it is.

Fatah   'Coarse and mundane at the same time, stories not fit for anyone's ears let alone a king –'

Zuya   Ungrateful little *sharmuta*.

Fatah   'Enjoy this – it'll be your last meal if you don't start weaving yarns that enchant and delight him – he's not just a cock.'

Akila *tears the paper into a hundred pieces and throws them up into the air like confetti. They all watch the finality of it.*

Akila   We stop. Leave Scheherazade to it. Let's see how she gets on without our help.

Naha   But what will we do? While we wait? For the inevitable. We need the stories . . . or we'll go . . . [mad]

Zuya   Need?

Fatah   Of course. It's our only escape.

Naha   We must keep on. Doesn't the King like our stories?

Wadiha   The guard says he hears him roaring with laughter – or groaning with ecstasy.

Naha   That might not be the stories . . .

Zuya   We should write back –

Fatah   Yeah – tell her to F– [fuck off]

Zuya *is impressed with* **Fatah***'s rage.*

Naha   No. We should respond with a story.

Zuya   About what?

Akila   No way. I'm not having anyone talk about my writing like that. Who does she think she is?

Zuya   You did say everyone is a critic – aren't you used to it yet? You need thicker skin.

Wadiha Wait, wait, listen – like I said the guard puts his ear to the door every night. They all do – love the stories Scheherazade tells. He says the King does too.

Naha Then why write the letter?

Zuya Maybe she's having a bad day and wanted to take it out on us?

Akila Fuck the bitch. If she's so high and mighty let's see how she manages on her own.

Zuya She's the sparrow! High and mighty! What happened to gratitude – to sisterhood?

Wadiha Sisterhood. Ha. It's a myth. Haven't you heard the story of the three sisters?

Naha Wait – Akila get the pen, Fatah the candle.

Akila But I'm not –

Naha The pen! Candle! – Go on, Wadiha.

Fatah *hands her the candle.*

Wadiha Three sisters lived in the countryside, they were poor but as close as three tamarind seeds in a pod.

Naha AKILA – WRITE, go on.

Reluctantly **Akila** *transcribes.*

Wadiha A good-looking bachelor lived nearby. He was a farmer, and owned a lot of land.

Zuya Sounds like a catch – where do I sign up?

Wadiha One day, out walking, the women sat down to rest in his field of courgettes, admiring their girth.

Naha Girth – *mabrouk*!

Wadiha 'What a fine man, with such natural bounty! Imagine the joy of being his wife,' they exclaimed. 'Why, if he asked for my hand,' said the eldest, loudly, 'I would make him so happy in the bedroom, he will spill tears of joy every time we make love.' 'If he asked to marry me,' said the middle sister, 'I would make him so happy in the kitchen, every meal he ate would cause him to sing with happiness.' The youngest and quietest of the three thought for a minute, for she was not such a good cook, nor was she particularly confident in her lovemaking abilities. 'If I were lucky enough to be his wife,' she said, 'I'd give him a daughter so precious, she'd be born with a ruby in her gum and a golden birthmark on her forehead.'

Little did they know that the owner of the land was up a tree, picking apples, and heard every word. Delighted, he proposed to all three and they accepted, overjoyed – 'How wonderful that we shall remain living together with this fine man!'

And so they married. But it was not long before the husband's post-coital cries of joy turned to non-committal grunts. And he soon began to grumble about the food that had once made him sing with happiness. *Walihi*, you women,' he said. 'What use are you to me?' By then it was time for the youngest sister to give birth – *mashallah*, a baby girl. The two eldest delivered her for their sister; it was a long and arduous labour. As they wrenched her from her mother they were dazzled by a bright light, a shining gold birthmark on her forehead. They checked her mouth with dread. Sure enough there was a small ruby nestled in her gum.

'You know what this means for us?' they cried. 'We'll be thrown out on our ears while she and her precious baby get everything.' So they chopped off the baby's little finger, and shoved it, bleeding, into her mother's mouth, while she slept. They gave the child to an old woman, who was passing through selling herbs, with strict instructions to bury her alive. Then they screamed as loud as they could in horror. The husband ran in. 'She ate her own child!' They cried, and pointed at the bloody finger in the mother's mouth as evidence. 'Is this true?' he asked. Broken-hearted, but with no recollection of what had happened, the poor mother had to concur that it must be. She was banished to the edge of his land, and forced to wear a dog's hide, and herd the goats in the field for the rest of her days.

Meanwhile the old woman took the girl back to the forest where she lived and brought her up as her own, for of course she couldn't bring herself to bury a baby alive. She named her Rabia, and the girl grew up, free and happy, wandering around the woods with her animal friends. But after a mere ten years, the old woman found herself at the end of her life. As she lay on her deathbed she told the girl the truth about her mother, her missing finger and the cruel trick her aunties had played.

Once the old woman had passed away young Rabia set off to find her real mother. She bought herself a fine headscarf in the hope of impressing her, and some beautiful robes to give to her as a present. She took with her on this journey a wolf, a sheep and a cat.

Off she went with her companions, and whomever she passed would cry, '*Ya*, Allah! A wolf, a sheep and a cat, and yet they don't fight?' '*Subhan* Allah!' Rabia would cry back. 'They are animals but capable of loving each other, and yet there once was a mother who ate her own child!' And everyone would reply, 'Really? What a strange tale', and Rabia would continue.

After some time Rabia arrived at her mother's village. There she met one of the farmhands, who exclaimed, '*Ya*, Allah! A wolf, a sheep and a cat, and yet they don't fight?' '*Subhan* Allah,' she replied. 'They are animals, but capable of loving each other, and yet there once was a mother who ate her own child!' 'Ah yes . . .' nodded the farmhand. 'I know the woman of whom you speak.'

Rabia begged him to show her where she lived. 'She's in that field right there!' said the farmhand. The girl looked, but all she could see was a dog chasing around after the goats. She looked again and realised, to her horror, that it was a woman, wearing a dog's hide, covered in dust and dirt, running around on all fours.

She went to speak to her. 'Is it true you ate your baby?' 'Apparently so,' nodded the woman with great sorrow, 'although I cannot remember such a horrific deed. I am now rightly condemned to living as a dog in this field.'

Rabia took her mother to the river, encouraged her to wash and gave her the clothes she had brought her. She was transformed. Then she took her mother to the farmer's house. Impressed by such a well-dressed and polite young woman, the farmer invited her in to dine with them. 'I would be delighted,' said Rabia, 'but I insist on bringing a guest.' 'By all means,' said the husband and was stunned to see his third wife, now out of her dog's hide, walking into his house. Neither he nor her two jealous sisters wanted to dine with the dog-woman, but none of them could refuse this smart newcomer.

They sat and enjoyed a fine meal. Rabia was a charming dinner guest and kept them all entertained with various tales as they ate. As they finished their final course of cakes and tea, she told them her last story. The one about the woman whose sisters were so jealous of her, they tricked her into believing she had eaten her own baby.

The mother gasped. The two wives nearly choked on their cakes. The husband cried, 'Impossible! Why I saw it with my own eyes – didn't I?' Rabia merely shrugged, and poured them all some more tea. They looked on, eyes wide, as they all noticed her missing finger at the same time.

Rabia looked up at them with a smile, displaying the ruby in her gum. 'Hot in here, isn't it?' she said, and took off her headscarf, dazzling them all with her golden birthmark. Her mother jumped to her feet, embracing her long-lost daughter, weeping tears of joy and gratitude.

The husband banished his two wives to the outer fields, forcing them to wear dog hides and herd goats until such time as they died of exhaustion – 'Come,' he said to his wife and child, 'at last we can be together as a family!'

'You must be joking,' said Rabia. 'After the way you've treated her?' 'She's right,' said the mother. 'You were quick to condemn and swift to punish. You've treated me cruelly for the last ten years. Enjoy your land and your goat-herding wives. Me and my girl are going to start living at last.'

And with that, the girl and her mother set off, travelling and busking with their entourage of animals, free as birds.

She blows out the candle.

A beat.

Fatah   I don't want us to wear dog hides.

Akila   Nor do I.

Fatah   I want to be free as birds . . .

Wadiha   Then we are agreed. This is our answer to Scheherazade – this story – we are all in this together. Because these stories are for us – all of us – not just her. Let's make a pact.

She puts her hand to her heart and they all touch it too.

While the hairs continue to grow on our head and we're above the ground not under it – we will write stories to save all our lives – we will stick together. Agreed?

All   Agreed.

Fatah   But what if [she betrays us] –

Wadiha   No – we can't doubt her – or ourselves. We must keep going . . . *yulla*!

They get back to work with urgency. Time passes.

Five Hundred Nights

They are all studiously working away at their stories. **Naha** *paces frustrated.*

Akila   Do you *have* to do that. It's distracting me.

Naha   I'm stuck. I don't know what she wants. This – character . . . People always *want* things in stories don't they?

Akila   Of course

Naha   How can I put myself in the mind of a young girl who *wants* to marry . . . it's just not me. Fatah, maybe you can help?

Fatah   Me? Naha, I spent my life trying to be a good girl. *Do* what was expected of me. What *they* wanted. I thought that was the right way to live . . . I never thought about what I wanted. I was so busy pleasing everyone else . . . And now what's going to happen to me . . . us . . . Imagine doing that to all those women, girls.

Zuya   Killing us.

Fatah   Yes.

Naha   He fucks us first.

Wadiha   Lucky us.

Fatah   He must really hate us all. All women.

Zuya   They all do – underneath it all. They don't trust us. You know what my husband once said to me – how am I supposed to trust an animal that bleeds every month but doesn't die.

Akila   We don't bleed anymore now though do we?

Naha   That's because we can't see the moon – the sky. He's turned everything upside down. Unnatural.

Fatah   Does that mean there will be no more children. Ever. That we are the last?

Zuya   Good. No more little bastard dictators running round killing everything.

Fatah   No more little girls. I always wanted a daughter . . .

Zuya   Why – why the hell would you want a daughter? When the world is the way it is. When we are treated like this. When she would have to endure all we've endured. Better never to have been born.

A beat.

Fatah (*to* **Zuya**)   He really said that? About bleeding once a month and not dying?

Wadiha   What a charmer . . . They're not all like that.

Zuya   The King is. My husband was. But we will get our revenge . . . like the fox and the wolf.

A beat as they look at her expectantly.

Wadiha (*handing her the* Hakawati's *lit candle*)   *Yulla*, tell it.

Zuya   So the fox and the wolf lived together. But it was *not* an easy match. The wolf was physically stronger and that made him the boss off all things in his mind. He bullied all the other animals, was mean and didn't share – he was generally loathed by all but no one had the guts to say anything to him because of his size and vile nature. Then one day the fox gathered all her strength and went to the wolf and warned him – mend your ways. Be kinder. Think of others and most of all stop talking with your fists. In reply the wolf belted the fox who was knocked clean out. She eventually came round and found herself apologising to the wolf – saying she shouldn't have provoked him. But with every word that came out of her mouth she hated him more and prayed and planned and connived to get her revenge. He would pay for what he had done.

Her opportunity came a few days later when, walking past a farm, she noticed a hole in the fence. She was starving and nearly darted straight through it to the hen house but something – a voice, the clever little voice in her head stopped her – 'Wait,' it said. 'Be cautious – nothing is ever this easy', and so she carefully approached the fence on her guard and of course her instincts were quite right. There – by the gap in the fence – was a trap. The farmer had dug a hole and covered it with some leaves so he could catch whatever beasts came to steal his chickens. The fox grasped her chance and ran back to the den where the wolf was sleeping. She told him that there was a hole in the fence and that she'd already had a bellyful – surely he'd like a feed too? The greedy wolf didn't need to be asked twice. He bolted to the fence and just as he passed through it fell into the famer's trap. At first he was furious with the fox shouting at her and ordering her to get him out. Then he wheedled – cried – asked for her to fetch his mother who would surely know what to do. He begged – bargained – offered the fox the den all to herself saying if she freed him he would disappear. The fox listened to all this smiling, then she threw her head back and called and screeched and wailed until the farmer and his family were alerted. They ran out to the trap and as they did the fox hid behind a tree watching them as they discovered the wolf – they gathered fistfuls of rocks, then threw them at him one by one and they crushed into his loathsome body – breaking his bones, drawing blood from his flesh, stoning him to death.

She blows out the candle.

The women step away from her, a little shocked.

Pause.

Naha   So much for a happy ending.

Zuya   No one said anything about a happy ending.

Akila   It's very – vivid.

Wadiha   Violent.

Fatah   Men are violent.

Zuya   Women can be violent too. Life is violent.

Naha   You're a widow, right?

Zuya   How did you guess?

Naha (*backing away from* **Zuya**, *understanding that she has committed violence*)   And your husband?

Zuya   Got what he deserved. I don't tell that story.

Akila   I think you already did.

Zuya   What?

Akila   Nothing.

Naha   Won't the King think the wolf is him and be angry?

Wadiha   Don't worry – no one ever notices themselves in stories. Trust me.

Akila   Naha has a point – whether he recognises himself or not that story is an invitation to violence . . . No, we cannot send it. We cannot send this story to Scheherazade. Get rid of it.

Zuya   Who made you the boss?

Akila   I'm the writer.

Zuya   We all are now. And that took me time. Effort.

Akila   It's completely irresponsible. Foxes getting revenge on wolves. It's transparent. But if she was kind – forgave him. Helped him out.

Zuya   NO, NO, NO! It's not your story to change.

Fatah   You're trying to censor her.

Akila   That's a big word for a little girl.

Naha   Don't patronise her.

Akila   This story will do too much damage. Change the ending or we are not sending it.

Wadiha   You're as bad as them. Why can't we win? Why do we have to be veiled – demure – beaten – subdued – why? ITS OUR TURN TO WIN.

Zuya   YES!

Akila   Because we don't want to provoke a bloodthirsty murderer into killing any more people. We are trying to subdue a lion.

Wadiha   We are lionesses!

Zuya   We will eat him alive! I will eat you alive!

She approaches **Akila** *ferociously and stands eye to eye with her threateningly. Who will blink first.* **Akila** *doesn't move.*

A beat.

Zuya   Fine – give me one of yours.

Akila   What?

Zuya   I'll change mine but I want to see one of yours – I want to see if I can improve it.

Akila   No.

Fatah   That's not fair. We are all equal here.

Wadiha   It seems some of us are more equal than others.

Akila   I'm a professional writer.

Zuya   Either you want our stories or not?

Akila   Of course I do –

Zuya   Then we need to be fair. We all need to have a voice. I'll change mine if you let me change one of yours.

Akila   I'm not comfortable with that.

Naha   Course not – it's your baby . . .

Zuya   Then I'm not comfortable with you censoring mine. You see this –

She pulls a hair from her head and burns it.

Zuya   And this –

She takes a page of her writing and burns it.

Zuya   Do you understand? It's the same. You erase my story you erase me.

Akila   Of course I understand – but THIS IS NOT A GAME, we are not children, these stories are not for kids. THIS IS LIFE OR DEATH. Keep your story. Tell it when the time is right, but now is not that time.

Zuya   But –

Akila   Writers have a responsibility.

Fatah   To the truth – we should tell the truth not lie to people. Not mislead or pretend. Even if the truth is bitter it's better than a life of lies.

Akila   Yes but there is a power in words. Stories. They must be told in the right way and at the right time.

Zuya   Who made you the arbiter – the censor?

Naha   Leave it, Zuya.

Zuya (*she swears roundly in Arabic*)   *Que summak sharmuta.*

Naha   We must stick together. Stay unified. Please . . . It's just a story.

Zuya   It's *my* story. And you know what, you *can't have it*. I *choose* not to send it I choose to keep it.

Akila   Thank you, Zuya.

Zuya   Fuck you, Akila.

An uneasy return to work. **Naha** *keeps a watch on* **Zuya** *in case she goes for* **Akila**. *Music signifies the passing of time. Perhaps there is a tally on the wall or the floor with chalk to denote how many nights have passed.*

One Thousand Nights

All the women are sat staring into space. Pens down. They are stuck. Blocked. Fucked.

Fatah *suddenly draws an in-breath as if inspiration has taken her. They all look at her expectantly, hopefully. She grabs a candle and moves to the centre of the stage – it seems as if she is about to tell a story.*

She breathes in and is about to speak but then slowly doubts herself, shakes her head and blows the candle out.

Everyone sighs, disappointed.

Fatah *returns to her place, depressed.*

Pause.

Zuya   There are no more left.

Wadiha   We've used them all up.

Naha   I knew this would happen.

Akila   He was right.

Fatah   Who?

Akila   Some old white guy. He said there are only seven kinds of story.

Fatah   Seven?

Akila   Overcoming the Monster. Rags to Riches. The Quest. Voyage and Return. Rebirth. Comedy. Tragedy. (*A beat.*) And we've told them all.

Wadiha   Hundreds of times.

Zuya   There's no more stories.

Akila   If that's true then what will I do? Writing is my job – there's nothing else for me!

Wadiha   You'll have to become a wife. Be happy with that. Like everyone else.

Fatah   I'll never get married. Never.

Zuya   You won't have a choice if / [Scheherazade fails]

Naha   Shh!

Fatah   When we get out of here

Akila   If –

Naha   That's right – believe, little one, believe . . .

Fatah   I'm going to travel the world. Explore places no one has ever discovered. No one will stop me.

Akila   We are never getting out of here. If the stories have run out then Scheherazade must fail. And we will all die. And when he's finished with the women in his country he will move on – his blood lust won't abate. He will travel to the next country and the next – marrying women and slaughtering us like animals – until there are no females left.

Pause as misery sets in.

Zuya   Bet you want my fox and wolf story now – but you can't have it.

Akila   ZUYA!

Wadiha   STOP it! Both of you!

Naha *gets up.*

Naha   I don't care about this seven stories ideas – we are chefs of words. We are magpies of literature, gatherers of meaning, magicians of text. And most of all we are thieves – we can whisk a story from right under your nose and deliver it back to you afresh . . . Like . . . like . . . like . . . (*eureka*) The thief and the donkey.

The women are alerted to the story coming – they are incandescent with anticipation. They grab a candle for her and light it as she continues.

All   Tell us – tell us, tell us, our *hakawati*!

Naha   There was once a thief so brilliant that she could steal the eyelashes off your face. She was challenged by another of her kind – who was nowhere as talented – to steal a donkey from a man who was passing. 'I can do it,' the great thief replied, 'but I need your help.' So the two thieves followed the man and the donkey quietly until they came to a fork in the road. There the great thief approached and quietly unbridled the donkey as he was being led – handed him over to the lesser thief who led him to the left fork and put the harness over her own head continuing with the owner to the right. A few minutes later when the man turned around to check his donkey he was amazed to see a woman in his place. 'Who are you?' he asked, and, 'Where is my donkey?' 'I'm afraid,' replied the thief, 'that I am your donkey. You see I have a terrible fondness for wine. And I overindulge. And one night I got so drunk that my father screamed and shouted at me when I got home – so I got a broom and beat him with it – I'm not proud of myself. He in return cursed me to heaven calling me a *h'mara*, a *hayawani*, and God was listening and turned me into a donkey. Next thing I know I'm being bought by you at the market. But today – today my father must have forgiven me and blessed me and so I've turned back into me.' The man was shocked and apologised for how hard he'd worked the woman when she was a donkey and sent the brilliant thief on her way. The thief had proven her cunning and skill.

Several days later she took the donkey to market to sell it, and while there the previous owner spotted the beast. As the thief hid she heard the man berate the animal, 'YOU'VE BEEN DRINKING AGAIN, HAVENT YOU? AND BEATING YOUR FATHER, YOU DEVIL.' The donkey recognised his old master and began to bray. 'BEG AS MUCH AS YOU LIKE, I'M NOT BUYING YOU AGAIN,' he replied.

The women all laugh so hard and gather round her to hug her.

Wadiha   And not a cock-sucking in sight, *mabrouk*!

Zuya   When she said donkey I did get worried . . .

They laugh and laugh, and blow her candle out with their laughter.

Music signifies the passing of time. Perhaps there is a tally on the wall or the floor with chalk to denote how many nights have passed.

One Thousand and One Nights

The women are all sat around writing. Working hard as usual. Suddenly the doors open. No one moves; they are too engrossed.

A beat.

Then **Fatah** *looks up.*

Fatah   The doors are open. EVERYONE – look!

They all look.

Fatah   What does it mean?

Wadiha   Someone's coming?

Fatah   Has he had enough of Scheherazade? Enough of her stories?

Naha   OH GOD, which of us will be next?

Fatah   Don't be scared

Zuya   NO ONE IS TAKING ANY OF US. COME HERE.

They stand together ready for the onslaught.

Zuya   We will be ready.

Pause. It's tense.

Nothing happens.

Fatah   What will happen?

Akila   Why is no one coming?

Zuya   I can't bear it – I'm going to find out.

Naha   Don't, Zuya, you might get in trouble.

Zuya   We are all threatened with death – what's worse than that?

She goes.

They all look anxious.

Wadiha   Maybe now is the time. Maybe now I'll get to do my dance . . . My last dance.

Akila   Can you remember how? We've been locked in here, writing stories for one thousand and one nights.

Wadiha   Forget dancing? Never. It presses to my memory. It's in my blood, my bones, my soul.

Music starts and she gets up and slowly looses her hair – she begins to do not a belly dance but a traditional Saudi Arabian hair dance. The other women watch on mesmerised – then join in one by one . . . it's a slow tune at first but the tempo rises and it gets faster and faster rising to a climax, as:

Zuya *re-enters – out of breath.*

Zuya   Stop!

The music and dancing stops suddenly.

Zuya   It's over! She did it.

Naha   She killed him?

Zuya   No, she made him love her. Want to keep her. He fell for all the stories . . .

A beat.

Zuya   *We* did it. IT'S OVER! WE'RE FREE! FREE!

Cheers and ululations as the women realise it's over.

They all head for the door.

Akila   Wait – wait – where are you going?

Naha   Didn't you hear her? We are free to go ! The stories worked.

Wadiha   The King is keeping Scheherazade – for good – and ending his tyrannical revenge.

Fatah   I can travel the world.

Zuya   I can join the army.

Naha   I'm going to buy a puppy . . .

Wadiha   And I'm going to set up my own dance studio. Women only.

Fatah   What about you, Akila? What will you do?

Akila   I'll do what I've always done. Go where it's safe. Here (*tapping her head*) and here (*indicating the page*).

Wadiha   Haven't you had enough of stories?

Akila   Not yet. And you know why – because every time I tell a story the chaos of the world stops. The mindless violence and unforgiving randomness, the torturous knife edge disappears. I am in control. Just for a few minutes. And everything makes sense. It's safe.

Naha   Sometimes stories can be scary. They can be bloody. Gruesome. They can get out of hand.

Akila   That's the power of the *Hakawati* to decide what happens. How it ends.

A beat.

Wadiha   Well, good luck.

They all go to leave.

Fatah   Wait. What about her?

Wadiha   Who? Scheherazade?

Fatah   Yes. We can't leave her.

Zuya   Why not?

Fatah   How can we be free if she's still captive?

Naha   He's her husband.

Fatah   He's a fucking murderer. We need to save her.

Naha   What if she doesn't want to be saved?

Zuya   She will want to be free. Everyone wants that. No one wants to be in a golden cage –

Fatah   like the sparrow,

Akila   or a golden lamp,

Fatah   like the jinni,

Wadiha   or a cell,

Fatah   like us – we need to find her.

Zuya   Yes. And ask her.

Naha   What?

Fatah   To tell us the end of the story. It's her turn.

A beat.

Fatah   Come on.

They join hands.

They exit.

The End.